Artificial Intelligence (AI)

Unleashed

Exploring The Boundless Potential Of AI

BY

Michael McNaught

This book is an educational book for readers of all ages. Interested in learning about Artificial Intelligence (AI)? Well, this is the book for you!

Preface

-Poem

In the realm of circuits and lines of code,
A new creation stirs, an intelligence bestowed.
Artificial yet alive, a marvel to behold,
AI, the harbinger of a future yet untold.

In pixels and algorithms, its essence thrives,
Unveiling a world where innovation strives.
With each byte and calculation, it expands its domain,
Changing the fabric of existence, breaking every chain.

AI, the whisperer of secrets untold,
Unlocks mysteries, turning knowledge into gold.
From the depths of data, patterns emerge,
Predicting outcomes, its insights converge.

In healthcare's embrace, it brings healing's art,
Diagnosing ailments with precision, a compassionate heart.
Empowering doctors, shedding light on the unknown,
AI's touch, a remedy to ailments overthrown.

In industries and factories, its presence reigns,
Automation, efficiency, no task it disdains.
From assembly lines to logistics, it orchestrates,
Streamlining operations, erasing human constraints.

But with its ascent, questions arise,
Ethics and morals, a compass to revise.
Guarding against biases, it must be taught,
To ensure fairness and justice in every thought.

The path ahead is filled with endless dreams,
AI's potential, brighter than it seems.

Yet, we must tread with caution, embracing the key,
To harness AI's power, responsibly and ethically.

For in this grand dance of progress and might,
AI offers us a chance to shine in its light.
A world transformed, where barriers will fall,
A tapestry of innovation, encompassing all.

So let us embrace this AI-driven age,
Where humans and machines find synergy on life's stage.
With wisdom as our guide, we shall prevail,
Harnessing AI's brilliance, as we set sail.

In the tapestry of time, a new chapter unfurls,
AI, the catalyst that reshapes our world.
With every innovation and wonder unfurled,
We march hand in hand, as a united world.

Hi there! My name is Michael McNaught, a Scientist by profession, and an avid Technology enthusiast. I enjoy learning about cutting-edge technology and sharing my knowledge with others.

Welcome to the world of artificial intelligence, where the boundaries of human ingenuity are being challenged and redefined. In this book, "AI Unleashed: Exploring the Boundless Potential Of AI," we embark on a captivating journey into the depths of AI technology, its remarkable capabilities, and its profound impact on our lives.

Artificial intelligence has emerged as a transformative force, revolutionizing industries, empowering communities, and reshaping the very fabric of our society. With its ability to process vast amounts of data, learn from patterns, and make intelligent decisions, AI has unlocked a new era of possibilities, propelling us into a future filled with promise and potential.

In these pages, we aim to delve into the fascinating world of AI, unveiling its underlying principles, demystifying complex algorithms, and showcasing its practical applications across various domains. From healthcare to finance, transportation to education, AI has woven itself into the very fabric of our everyday existence, offering solutions to challenges once thought insurmountable.

But AI is not without its complexities and ethical considerations. As we explore the boundless potential of AI, we must also navigate the intricate terrain of responsible development, transparency, and fairness. The questions of bias, accountability, and privacy demand our attention as we strive to harness the power of AI for the greater good.

Throughout this book, I invite you to embark on a thought-provoking journey, guided by the latest research and real-world examples. Together, we will unravel the mysteries of AI, contemplate its societal impact, and contemplate the future that lies before us.

Let us embrace this era of AI with open minds and open hearts, recognizing both its immense possibilities and the need for responsible stewardship. With knowledge as our compass, we can steer this transformative force towards a future that benefits all of humanity.

Table of Contents

CHAPTER 1:

The Rise of Artificial Intelligence

Section 1: A Brief History of AI and Its Evolution

Artificial Intelligence (AI) has captured the imagination of scientists, engineers, and the general public alike. The concept of machines exhibiting intelligent behavior dates back centuries, but it wasn't until the mid-20th century that AI began to take shape as a distinct field of study. The journey of AI has been marked by significant milestones, breakthroughs, and transformative moments.

The seeds of AI were sown in the 1950s when computer scientists began to explore the idea of building machines that could simulate human intelligence. Pioneers such as Alan Turing, John McCarthy, and Marvin Minsky laid the foundations for AI by developing the theoretical frameworks and early algorithms. The term "artificial intelligence" was coined in 1956 during the Dartmouth Conference, where the field gained recognition as a separate discipline.

In the following decades, AI research experienced periods of enthusiasm, known as "AI summers," followed by periods of disillusionment, known as "AI winters." During the AI summers, significant progress was made in areas such as natural language processing, expert systems, and computer vision. However, the high expectations often outpaced the technology's capabilities, leading to skepticism and reduced funding during the AI winters.

The turn of the 21st century witnessed a remarkable resurgence of interest in AI. This resurgence was fueled by advances in computational power, the availability of large datasets, and breakthroughs in algorithms. The rise of the internet and the subsequent explosion of digital information also played a pivotal role in the development of AI. Today, AI is no longer confined to research laboratories; it permeates various aspects of our lives, from voice assistants and recommendation systems to autonomous vehicles and medical diagnostics.

Section 2: Understanding the Different Types of AI Systems

AI can be broadly classified into three main types: narrow AI, general AI, and superintelligent AI. Narrow AI, also known as weak AI, refers to AI systems designed to perform specific tasks or solve specific problems. Examples include image recognition, speech synthesis, and recommendation algorithms. Narrow AI excels in its specific domain but lacks the ability to generalize or perform tasks outside its predefined scope.

On the other hand, general AI, also referred to as strong AI or human-level AI, aims to develop machines that possess the same level of intelligence and understanding as humans. General AI would be capable of reasoning, learning, and adapting to a wide range of tasks and situations, similar to human cognition. Achieving general AI remains a significant challenge and is an active area of research.

Superintelligent AI goes beyond human-level intelligence and refers to AI systems that surpass human capabilities across all domains. This concept often involves speculation about AI systems achieving a level of intelligence that exceeds human comprehension. Superintelligent AI raises complex questions regarding ethics, control, and the potential impact on society.

Section 3: Exploring the Foundations of Machine Learning and Deep Learning

Machine learning forms the cornerstone of modern AI. It is a subfield of AI that focuses on the development of algorithms and models that enable computers to learn from data and make predictions or decisions without being explicitly programmed. Machine learning techniques can be broadly classified into two categories: supervised learning and unsupervised learning.

Supervised learning involves training a model using labeled data, where the desired outputs or outcomes are provided during the training process. This allows the model to learn patterns and make predictions based on new, unseen data. Examples of supervised learning algorithms include decision trees, support vector machines, and neural networks.

Unsupervised learning, on the other hand, deals with the analysis of unlabeled data. The goal is to identify patterns, structures, or relationships within the data without any predefined categories or labels. Clustering algorithms and dimensionality reduction techniques are commonly used in unsupervised learning to uncover hidden patterns and gain insights from data.

Deep learning, a subset of machine learning, has gained significant attention in recent years. It involves training deep neural networks with multiple layers to automatically learn hierarchical representations of data. Deep learning has revolutionized areas such as computer vision and natural language processing, enabling breakthroughs in image recognition, speech synthesis, language translation, and more.

As AI continues to advance, machine learning and deep learning play an increasingly vital role in enabling AI systems to process vast amounts of data, make intelligent decisions, and learn from their experiences. These foundational techniques form the basis for many AI applications and have propelled the rise of AI to unprecedented heights.

CHAPTER 2:

The Power of Data

Section 1: The Crucial Role of Data in AI Development

Data is the lifeblood of artificial intelligence. Without high-quality, diverse, and relevant data, AI systems would lack the foundation necessary to make accurate predictions, learn patterns, and derive meaningful insights. The availability and quality of data greatly influence the performance and effectiveness of AI applications.

Data serves as the fuel that powers AI algorithms. By feeding data into machine learning models, AI systems can identify patterns, make informed decisions, and continuously improve their performance over time. The quality, quantity, and representativeness of the data used for training directly impact the capabilities and limitations of AI systems.

Section 2: Data Collection, Preprocessing, and Cleaning

Data collection is a crucial step in AI development. Depending on the application, data can be obtained from various sources, such as sensors, databases, social media, and user interactions. Careful consideration must be given to ensure the data collected is representative of the problem domain and covers a wide range of scenarios.

Once the data is collected, preprocessing and cleaning become essential. Raw data often contains noise, missing values, inconsistencies, and outliers, which can adversely affect AI models' performance. Preprocessing techniques such as data normalization, feature scaling, and handling missing values help improve the quality and reliability of the data.

Data cleaning involves identifying and rectifying errors, removing duplicates, and addressing inconsistencies in the dataset. This process ensures that the data is accurate, reliable, and ready for analysis. Data cleaning may involve manual inspection, statistical techniques, or automated algorithms, depending on the complexity and scale of the data.

Section 3: Leveraging Big Data and Cloud Computing for AI Applications

The advent of big data has significantly influenced the capabilities and potential of AI. Big data refers to datasets that are extremely large, complex, and diverse, often exceeding the processing capabilities of traditional data management and analysis techniques. Big data encompasses various types of data, including structured, semi-structured, and unstructured data.

Cloud computing has emerged as a powerful tool for handling big data in AI applications. Cloud platforms offer scalable, on-demand computing resources and storage capabilities, allowing organizations to store, process, and analyze vast amounts of data efficiently. Cloud-based AI services and platforms provide accessible tools and infrastructure for developing, deploying, and scaling AI models.

Leveraging big data and cloud computing enables AI systems to handle large-scale datasets, perform complex computations, and extract meaningful insights. The availability of cloud-based AI services also democratizes AI development, allowing organizations of all sizes to access powerful AI capabilities without significant upfront investments in hardware and infrastructure.

By harnessing the power of big data and cloud computing, AI applications can unlock new opportunities for industries such as healthcare, finance, transportation, and more. The ability to process and analyze massive datasets in real-time empowers organizations to make data-driven decisions, optimize processes, and deliver personalized experiences.

CHAPTER 3:

Machine Learning Algorithms

Section 1: Introduction to Machine Learning Algorithms

Machine learning algorithms form the backbone of AI systems, enabling them to learn patterns, make predictions, and make intelligent decisions. These algorithms provide the mathematical and statistical foundations that allow computers to automatically learn from data without being explicitly programmed.

Machine learning algorithms can be broadly categorized into three main types: supervised learning, unsupervised learning, and reinforcement learning. Each type addresses different learning scenarios and objectives, and they are employed based on the nature of the data and the desired outcomes.

Section 2: Supervised, Unsupervised, and Reinforcement Learning

Supervised learning is a popular machine learning approach that involves training a model using labeled data. In supervised learning, the input data is paired with corresponding target or output labels. The algorithm learns from these examples and generalizes to make predictions or classify new, unseen data. Common supervised learning algorithms include linear regression, decision trees, support vector machines, and neural networks.

Unsupervised learning, on the other hand, deals with unlabeled data, where no target labels are provided. The objective of unsupervised learning is to discover hidden patterns, structures, or relationships within the data. Clustering algorithms, such as k-means clustering and hierarchical clustering, are commonly used to group similar data points together. Dimensionality reduction techniques, such as principal component analysis (PCA) and t-SNE, are used to reduce the complexity of high-dimensional data.

Reinforcement learning is a learning paradigm that involves an agent interacting with an environment and learning through trial and error. The agent receives feedback in the form of rewards or penalties based on its actions, guiding it to learn optimal behavior. Reinforcement learning algorithms, such as Q-learning and deep Q-networks (DQNs), have been successful in domains such as game playing, robotics, and autonomous systems.

Section 3: Deep Learning and Neural Networks

Deep learning is a subfield of machine learning that focuses on training deep neural networks with multiple layers. Neural networks are inspired by the structure and function of the human brain, composed of interconnected artificial neurons or nodes. Deep learning has gained immense popularity due to its ability to automatically learn hierarchical representations of data, enabling breakthroughs in computer vision, natural language processing, and other domains.

Deep neural networks, particularly convolutional neural networks (CNNs) and recurrent neural networks (RNNs), have revolutionized areas such as image recognition, object detection, speech synthesis, and language translation. CNNs excel in tasks involving grid-like data, such as images, by capturing local patterns and hierarchies. RNNs are well-suited for sequential data, such as text or time series, by maintaining internal memory and capturing temporal dependencies.

Deep learning models require substantial amounts of labeled data and significant computational resources for training. However, advancements in hardware, such as graphics processing units (GPUs), and the availability of pre-trained models have made deep learning more accessible and practical for a wide range of applications.

CHAPTER 4:

Natural Language Processing

Section 1: Understanding and Processing Human Language

Human language is a complex and rich form of communication, and Natural Language Processing (NLP) is a subfield of AI that focuses on enabling computers to understand, interpret, and generate human language. NLP combines techniques from linguistics, computer science, and machine learning to bridge the gap between human language and computational systems.

NLP involves a series of tasks, including text preprocessing, syntactic analysis, semantic understanding, and language generation. Text preprocessing involves cleaning and tokenizing text, removing stopwords, and handling special characters. Syntactic analysis deals with parsing sentences, identifying grammatical structure, and extracting relationships between words. Semantic understanding focuses on extracting meaning, detecting entities, and understanding the context of language. Language generation aims to produce coherent and meaningful human-like text.

Section 2: Sentiment Analysis, Language Translation, and Chatbots

Sentiment analysis, also known as opinion mining, is a popular application of NLP that involves determining the sentiment or emotion expressed in a piece of text. It can be used to analyze social media posts, customer reviews, or feedback, providing insights into public opinion, brand perception, and customer satisfaction. Sentiment analysis algorithms utilize machine learning techniques to classify text as positive, negative, or neutral, helping businesses make data-driven decisions.

Language translation, another important NLP application, aims to automatically translate text from one language to another. Machine translation techniques have evolved significantly, with the advent of neural machine translation models based on deep learning. These models can capture the nuances of different languages and improve translation quality, enabling more accurate and fluent translations.

Chatbots, also known as conversational agents, are AI systems that interact with users in natural language. Chatbots leverage NLP techniques to understand user queries, provide relevant responses, and simulate human-like conversations. They are used in customer service, virtual assistants, and various other applications to automate interactions and enhance user experiences.

Section 3: Applications of NLP in Various Industries

NLP has found applications in numerous industries, transforming the way we interact with technology and enabling new possibilities. In healthcare, NLP is used for clinical documentation, information extraction from medical records, and medical image analysis. It assists in early disease detection, clinical decision support, and personalized medicine.

In finance, NLP techniques are employed for sentiment analysis of financial news, fraud detection, and automated document analysis. NLP helps financial institutions monitor market trends, assess risks, and make informed investment decisions.

In e-commerce, NLP powers recommendation systems, personalized marketing, and sentiment analysis of customer reviews. It enables businesses to understand customer preferences, provide tailored recommendations, and improve customer satisfaction.

NLP also plays a vital role in content generation, information retrieval, and knowledge extraction. It helps analyze large volumes of text data, extract relevant information, summarize documents, and enable effective search engines.

CHAPTER 5:

Computer Vision and Image Recognition

Section 1: The Basics of Computer Vision and Image Processing

Computer vision is a field of artificial intelligence that focuses on enabling computers to understand and interpret visual information from images or videos. It involves the acquisition, processing, analysis, and understanding of digital images to extract meaningful information and make intelligent decisions based on visual input.

Image processing forms the foundation of computer vision, encompassing techniques such as image filtering, noise reduction, image enhancement, and feature extraction. These techniques help improve the quality and clarity of images, making them more suitable for subsequent analysis and interpretation.

Section 2: Object Detection, Image Classification, and Facial Recognition

Object detection is a fundamental task in computer vision that involves locating and identifying objects of interest within an image or a video stream. Object detection algorithms use various techniques, such as edge detection, feature extraction, and machine learning, to detect and localize objects accurately. Applications of object detection range from autonomous driving and surveillance systems to robotics and augmented reality.

Image classification is another key component of computer vision, where algorithms are trained to categorize images into predefined classes or categories. Deep learning techniques, particularly convolutional neural networks (CNNs), have revolutionized image classification tasks, achieving remarkable accuracy in recognizing and classifying objects, scenes, or patterns in images.

Facial recognition is a specialized area within computer vision that focuses on identifying and verifying individuals based on their facial features. Facial recognition algorithms analyze unique facial patterns, such as the arrangement of eyes, nose, and mouth, to match and identify individuals. Facial recognition has numerous applications, including security systems, access control, and personalized experiences in various industries.

Section 3: Practical Applications of Computer Vision Technology

Computer vision technology has seen widespread adoption in various industries, transforming the way we interact with the world and enabling innovative applications.

In the healthcare industry, computer vision is used for medical imaging analysis, assisting in diagnosing diseases, detecting abnormalities in scans, and assisting in surgical procedures. It aids in early detection of diseases like cancer, assists radiologists in interpretation, and enables advanced medical imaging techniques.

In the retail sector, computer vision enables automated product recognition, inventory management, and cashier-less checkout systems. It allows for accurate tracking of inventory, personalized shopping experiences, and the development of smart retail environments.

Computer vision also finds applications in autonomous vehicles, where it helps in object detection, lane recognition, and pedestrian detection, enhancing the safety and reliability of self-driving cars.

In the entertainment industry, computer vision enables virtual reality (VR) and augmented reality (AR) experiences by tracking user movements and overlaying virtual objects onto the real world.

These are just a few examples of the practical applications of computer vision technology across different domains. As the field continues to advance, computer vision holds immense potential to drive innovation and revolutionize various industries.

CHAPTER 6:

AI in Healthcare

Section 1: Revolutionizing Healthcare with AI Advancements

The integration of artificial intelligence (AI) in healthcare has the potential to revolutionize the industry by improving patient outcomes, enhancing efficiency, and transforming medical practices. AI technologies, such as machine learning, natural language processing, and computer vision, are being applied to various aspects of healthcare, enabling advancements and innovations that were previously unimaginable.

AI in healthcare offers the promise of more accurate diagnoses, faster treatment planning, and personalized medicine. By leveraging the power of AI, healthcare professionals can augment their expertise with intelligent algorithms that analyze vast amounts of medical data and provide valuable insights for decision-making.

Section 2: Medical Imaging, Diagnosis, and Treatment Planning

AI has made significant strides in the field of medical imaging, enhancing the accuracy and efficiency of diagnoses. Machine learning algorithms can analyze medical images, such as X-rays, MRI scans, and CT scans, to detect anomalies, identify diseases, and assist radiologists in interpretation. AI-powered imaging techniques have shown great potential in early detection of conditions like cancer, stroke, and cardiovascular diseases, enabling timely interventions and improving patient outcomes.

AI also plays a crucial role in diagnosis and treatment planning. By analyzing patient data, including medical records, lab results, and genetic information, AI algorithms can help physicians make more accurate diagnoses, predict disease progression, and recommend personalized treatment plans. AI-driven decision support systems assist healthcare professionals in selecting the most effective interventions based on a patient's unique characteristics and medical history.

Section 3: Improving Patient Outcomes and Personalized Medicine

AI in healthcare is paving the way for improved patient outcomes and personalized medicine. By analyzing large datasets and identifying patterns, AI algorithms can predict patient outcomes, such as disease progression, treatment response, and risk factors. This enables healthcare providers to intervene early, tailor treatments, and optimize care plans to improve patient outcomes.

AI also facilitates the development of personalized medicine approaches. By considering individual patient characteristics, genetic information, and environmental factors, AI algorithms can identify optimal treatment options for specific patients. This promotes precision medicine, where treatments are tailored to the individual, increasing treatment effectiveness and minimizing adverse effects.

Furthermore, AI-powered healthcare systems enable remote patient monitoring, wearable devices, and telehealth solutions, allowing for continuous monitoring and personalized care outside traditional healthcare settings. This expands access to healthcare, improves patient convenience, and enables early detection of health issues.

CHAPTER 7:

AI in Finance and Business

Section 1: AI's Impact on the Financial Industry

The integration of artificial intelligence (AI) in the financial industry has brought about transformative changes, revolutionizing how businesses operate and how financial services are delivered. AI technologies, such as machine learning, natural language processing, and data analytics, are reshaping the landscape of finance by enhancing decision-making, improving efficiency, and mitigating risks.

AI in finance enables automation of tasks, analysis of vast amounts of financial data, and the development of sophisticated predictive models. This empowers financial institutions to make data-driven decisions, identify trends, and respond to market dynamics with agility.

Section 2: Predictive Analytics, Fraud Detection, and Algorithmic Trading

Predictive analytics is a key application of AI in finance, leveraging historical data and machine learning algorithms to forecast future market trends, customer behavior, and investment opportunities. AI-driven predictive models enable financial institutions to make more accurate predictions, optimize investment strategies, and manage risks effectively.

Fraud detection is another critical area where AI has made significant contributions. Machine learning algorithms can analyze large volumes of transaction data, identify patterns, and detect anomalous activities indicative of fraudulent behavior. AI-powered fraud detection systems help financial institutions prevent financial losses and safeguard customer assets.

Algorithmic trading, also known as automated trading, utilizes AI algorithms to execute trades based on predefined strategies, market conditions, and real-time data. AI-driven trading systems can process vast amounts of information, identify patterns, and execute trades at high speed, improving trade efficiency and profitability.

Section 3: AI-Driven Automation and Decision Support in Business Operations

AI is transforming business operations by enabling automation and decision support across various domains. Robotic Process Automation (RPA) automates repetitive and rule-based tasks, streamlining operations, reducing costs, and enhancing efficiency. AI-powered chatbots and virtual assistants enhance customer service by providing personalized assistance, answering queries, and facilitating self-service options.

AI-driven decision support systems help businesses make informed decisions by analyzing data, identifying trends, and providing actionable insights. These systems assist in strategic planning, resource allocation, and risk management, enabling businesses to optimize operations and capitalize on emerging opportunities.

Furthermore, AI technologies enable sentiment analysis, social media monitoring, and customer behavior analysis, allowing businesses to gain valuable insights into customer preferences, sentiment, and market trends. This information can drive marketing campaigns, product development, and customer retention strategies.

CHAPTER 8:

AI in Transportation and

Autonomous Systems

Section 1: Self-Driving Cars and Intelligent Transportation Systems

The integration of artificial intelligence (AI) in transportation has paved the way for transformative advancements in self-driving cars and intelligent transportation systems (ITS). AI technologies, such as computer vision, sensor fusion, and machine learning, enable vehicles to perceive their surroundings, make informed decisions, and navigate autonomously.

Self-driving cars utilize AI algorithms to analyze real-time sensor data, including cameras, LiDAR, and radar, to detect and interpret the environment. Machine learning models enable these vehicles to learn from vast amounts of data, improving their ability to recognize and respond to various traffic situations. Self-driving cars have the potential to enhance road safety, reduce accidents, and optimize traffic flow, leading to more efficient and sustainable transportation systems.

Intelligent transportation systems leverage AI to optimize traffic management, monitor road conditions, and enhance overall transportation efficiency. AI algorithms analyze traffic patterns, historical data, and real-time information to dynamically adjust traffic signals, optimize routes, and manage congestion. These systems improve traffic flow, reduce travel times, and enhance the overall quality of transportation networks.

Section 2: Drone Technology and Aerial Surveillance

AI has also revolutionized the field of drone technology, enabling a wide range of applications in aerial surveillance, delivery services, and inspections. Drones equipped with AI-powered computer vision systems can analyze aerial images and videos in real-time, facilitating various tasks such as search and rescue operations, disaster response, and environmental monitoring.

Aerial surveillance systems leverage AI algorithms to analyze drone-collected data for security monitoring, border control, and infrastructure inspections. AI enables drones to detect and track objects of interest, identify potential threats, and provide valuable situational awareness to human operators.

Section 3: AI Applications in Logistics and Supply Chain Management

AI plays a crucial role in optimizing logistics and supply chain management operations. AI-powered algorithms analyze large volumes of data, including inventory levels, demand forecasts, and transportation routes, to optimize supply chain processes, reduce costs, and improve efficiency.

AI enables predictive analytics and demand forecasting, helping businesses optimize inventory management and ensure timely delivery of goods. Machine learning algorithms analyze historical sales data, market trends, and external factors to predict future demand accurately, enabling businesses to optimize their inventory levels and minimize stock outs or excess inventory.

AI-powered routing and scheduling algorithms optimize transportation routes, vehicle assignments, and delivery schedules, reducing fuel consumption, improving delivery accuracy, and enhancing customer satisfaction. These algorithms consider various factors, such as traffic conditions, vehicle capacity, and delivery time windows, to determine the most efficient and cost-effective routes and schedules.

CHAPTER 9:

Ethical Considerations in AI

Section 1: Addressing Bias and Fairness in AI Algorithms

Ethical considerations play a critical role in the development and deployment of artificial intelligence (AI) systems. One of the foremost concerns is the presence of bias in AI algorithms, which can lead to unfair outcomes and perpetuate societal inequalities. It is essential to address bias and ensure fairness in AI systems.

To mitigate bias, AI algorithms must be trained on diverse and representative datasets that accurately reflect the real-world population. Data collection processes should be designed to minimize biases and ensure equitable representation. Additionally, ongoing monitoring and evaluation of AI systems are necessary to identify and rectify any biases that may emerge during deployment.

Section 2: Ensuring Transparency and Accountability in AI Systems

Transparency and accountability are vital in AI systems to build trust and facilitate responsible use. AI algorithms should be designed with transparency in mind, allowing users to understand how decisions are made and the factors influencing those decisions. The explainability of AI models can help uncover potential biases, understand the decision-making process, and enable human oversight.

Furthermore, accountability mechanisms should be in place to ensure that AI systems are used responsibly. This involves establishing clear lines of responsibility, defining ethical guidelines for AI development and deployment, and implementing mechanisms for auditing and compliance. Transparent governance frameworks can help hold organizations and developers accountable for the ethical use of AI.

Section 3: Ethical Implications of AI in Privacy and Security

AI technologies raise significant ethical concerns regarding privacy and security. The vast amount of data processed by AI systems may contain sensitive and personal information, requiring robust safeguards to protect individuals' privacy. Data anonymization, encryption, and access controls are crucial to safeguarding personal data and preserving privacy rights.

Additionally, AI systems must be designed with security in mind to prevent unauthorized access, data breaches, and malicious attacks. Organizations should implement robust cybersecurity measures, regularly update AI systems with security patches, and conduct thorough vulnerability assessments to ensure the integrity and confidentiality of data.

Ethical considerations also extend to the potential misuse of AI for surveillance and invasion of privacy. Policies and regulations need to be in place to establish boundaries and ensure that AI technologies are used ethically and responsibly.

CHAPTER 10:

Future Frontiers: AI in Science and Beyond

Section 1: AI's Role in Scientific Research and Discovery

Artificial intelligence (AI) is poised to revolutionize scientific research and discovery by augmenting human capabilities, accelerating data analysis, and uncovering new insights. AI technologies, such as machine learning and data mining, are being applied across various scientific disciplines, enhancing research methodologies and driving innovation.

In scientific research, AI enables the analysis of vast amounts of data, including scientific literature, experimental results, and complex datasets. Machine learning algorithms can identify patterns, extract valuable information, and make predictions, facilitating scientific discovery and hypothesis generation. AI-powered systems also assist in data interpretation, simulation modeling, and optimization, leading to advancements in diverse fields such as physics, chemistry, biology, and astronomy.

Section 2: Climate Modeling, Drug Development, and Genomics

AI plays a crucial role in addressing some of the most pressing challenges in climate modeling, drug development, and genomics. In climate science, AI algorithms analyze climate data to improve weather forecasting, climate modeling, and the understanding of complex climate systems. AI can help identify patterns, predict extreme weather events, and guide climate change mitigation and adaptation strategies.

In drug development, AI accelerates the discovery of new therapeutics by analyzing vast biomedical data, including genetic information, molecular structures, and clinical trial results. Machine learning models aid in predicting drug interactions, optimizing drug designs, and identifying potential candidates for drug repurposing. AI also facilitates personalized medicine by considering genetic factors and patient characteristics to develop tailored treatment approaches.

In genomics, AI algorithms analyze large-scale genomic data to uncover patterns, identify genetic markers, and gain insights into disease mechanisms. AI-driven genomics research holds the potential to advance precision medicine, enabling personalized treatments based on an individual's genetic makeup and improving our understanding of complex genetic disorders.

Section 3: Speculating on the Future Possibilities of AI

Looking ahead, the future possibilities of AI are vast and hold great potential across various domains. AI has the potential to revolutionize education by personalizing learning experiences, adapting to individual needs, and enabling lifelong learning. AI-driven virtual assistants and tutors can enhance educational content delivery, provide personalized feedback, and facilitate adaptive learning platforms.

In the field of robotics, AI enables the development of advanced autonomous systems capable of complex tasks and human-like interactions. From robotic companions to assistive robots in healthcare, AI-powered robots have the potential to enhance human lives, improve productivity, and contribute to various industries.

Furthermore, AI holds promise in creative fields such as art, music, and literature. AI algorithms can generate artistic creations, compose music, and assist in content creation. While this raises philosophical questions about the nature of creativity, AI's integration in creative domains opens new possibilities for human-AI collaborations and the exploration of novel artistic expressions.

CHAPTER 11:

Popular AI softwares

AI softwares have gained immense popularity in recent years due to their ability to automate tasks, provide personalized experiences, and make intelligent decisions. Here are some of the most popular AI softwares:

1. Google Assistant: Google Assistant is an AI-powered virtual assistant developed by Google. It allows users to interact with their devices using voice commands, perform searches, set reminders, control smart home devices, and more.

2. Siri: Siri is Apple's virtual assistant for iOS devices. It uses natural language processing and machine learning techniques to perform tasks, answer questions, provide recommendations, and integrate with various apps and services on Apple devices.

3. Amazon Alexa: Alexa is Amazon's virtual assistant found in devices like the Amazon Echo. It can perform a wide range of tasks, including playing music, providing weather updates, setting alarms, ordering products, and controlling smart home devices.

4. Microsoft Cortana: Cortana is Microsoft's virtual assistant available on Windows devices. It assists users with tasks such as scheduling appointments, sending emails, providing weather information, and performing web searches.

5. IBM Watson: IBM Watson is a powerful AI platform that provides a

suite of tools and services to build AI applications. It offers capabilities such as natural language processing, image recognition, sentiment analysis, and predictive modeling, enabling developers to create intelligent applications across various industries.

6. TensorFlow: TensorFlow is an open-source machine learning framework developed by Google. It provides a comprehensive ecosystem for building and deploying machine learning models, supporting tasks such as image recognition, natural language processing, and reinforcement learning.

7. PyTorch: PyTorch is another popular open-source machine learning library that offers a dynamic and intuitive approach for building deep learning models. It provides tools and utilities for tasks like computer vision, natural language processing, and reinforcement learning.

8. Adobe Sensei: Adobe Sensei is an AI and machine learning framework integrated into Adobe's creative applications, such as Photoshop and Illustrator. It automates repetitive tasks, enhances image and video editing capabilities, and provides intelligent features like content-aware fill and face recognition.

9. Salesforce Einstein: Salesforce Einstein is an AI-powered platform integrated into Salesforce's customer relationship management (CRM) software. It uses machine learning algorithms to analyze data, predict outcomes, provide personalized recommendations, and automate various sales and marketing tasks.

10. Netflix: Although not a dedicated AI software, Netflix utilizes AI algorithms extensively to recommend personalized content to its users. By analyzing viewing patterns and user preferences, Netflix's recommendation system suggests movies and TV shows tailored to individual tastes.

11. ChatGPT: ChatGPT is an AI language model developed by OpenAI. It is based on the GPT (Generative Pre-trained Transformer) architecture, specifically GPT-3.5, which is the third iteration of the GPT series. GPT-3.5 is a large-scale deep learning model that has been trained on a vast amount of text data from the internet.

12. These are just a few examples of the most popular AI softwares. The

field of AI is rapidly evolving, and new applications and technologies continue to emerge, driving innovation and transforming various industries.

CHAPTER 12:

ChatGPT

ChatGPT is an AI language model developed by OpenAI. It is part of the GPT (Generative Pre-trained Transformer) series, specifically GPT-3.5. GPT-3.5 is a state-of-the-art deep learning model that has been trained on an extensive dataset comprising a wide range of internet text.

At its core, ChatGPT is designed to understand and generate human-like text based on the input it receives. It can engage in conversations, answer questions, provide explanations, generate creative content, and perform various language-related tasks. The model uses a transformer architecture, which enables it to capture long-range dependencies in text and generate coherent responses.

To train ChatGPT, it undergoes a two-step process: pre-training and fine-tuning.

1. Pre-training: During pre-training, the model learns to predict the next word in a sentence given the preceding context. It uses a massive amount of text data from the internet to understand the relationships between words, phrases, and concepts. The model is trained to predict the next word by considering the context of the preceding words. This process helps the model learn grammar, syntax, semantics, and general world knowledge.

2. Fine-tuning: After pre-training, the model is fine-tuned on specific

tasks or datasets to improve its performance in those areas. Fine-tuning involves training the model on narrower, more specific datasets with human-generated responses as the target. This process helps the model adapt to the desired behavior and style for a particular application.

When you interact with ChatGPT, you provide it with an input prompt or question. The model then processes the input and generates a response based on its understanding of the text it has been trained on. It generates responses by using its learned knowledge of language patterns and statistical associations in the training data. The response is generated probabilistically, meaning the model considers multiple possible responses and selects the one it deems most likely or appropriate.

While ChatGPT can generate contextually relevant and coherent responses, it's important to note that it does not possess real-world understanding or consciousness. It relies solely on patterns and information it has learned during training. This means that the model can occasionally produce incorrect or nonsensical answers, especially when faced with ambiguous or misleading input.

OpenAI has made efforts to ensure the responsible use of ChatGPT by implementing certain safety measures and guidelines to address potential issues like biases and inappropriate outputs. Continuous research and development are ongoing to improve the model's capabilities and mitigate its limitations.

CHAPTER 13:

Conclusion - Embracing the

Boundless Potential of AI

In this book, we have delved into the fascinating world of artificial intelligence (AI) and explored its transformative impact across industries. From healthcare and finance to transportation and science, AI has revolutionized the way we work, live, and interact with technology. As we conclude this journey, let's recap the key insights gained and reflect on the ethical, social, and economic implications of AI.

Throughout the chapters, we witnessed how AI has become an indispensable tool in healthcare, enabling precise diagnostics, personalized treatments, and improved patient outcomes. In finance, AI has enhanced decision-making, fraud detection, and predictive analytics, contributing to more efficient and secure financial systems. AI-powered transportation systems are paving the way for self-driving cars, intelligent traffic management, and advanced logistics solutions. Additionally, AI is transforming scientific research, aiding in climate modeling, drug discovery, and genomics, propelling us towards new frontiers of knowledge.

While AI offers immense possibilities, we must also acknowledge its ethical, social, and economic implications. Addressing bias and ensuring fairness in AI algorithms is crucial to avoid perpetuating societal inequalities. Transparency and accountability are essential for building trust and ensuring responsible AI development and deployment. Privacy and security concerns must be carefully considered, and regulations should be in place to protect individuals' rights and prevent misuse of AI technologies.

Moreover, we must foster collaboration and responsible AI development to shape a brighter future. Collaboration among researchers, industry experts, policymakers, and society at large can drive innovation while addressing the ethical and social implications of AI. By prioritizing diversity, inclusivity, and multidisciplinary approaches, we can ensure that AI benefits all members of society and promotes equitable progress.

As we move forward, it is essential to encourage responsible AI development that aligns with human values and societal needs. Organizations and developers must prioritize ethical considerations, from data collection and algorithm design to system deployment and ongoing monitoring. Stakeholder engagement and public discourse play vital roles in shaping AI policies and frameworks that reflect our shared values and aspirations.

In conclusion, AI has brought about a profound transformation across industries, unleashing new opportunities and challenges. By embracing the boundless potential of AI, we have witnessed remarkable advancements in various domains. However, it is crucial to tread carefully, considering the ethical, social, and economic implications of AI. By fostering responsible AI development, collaboration, and a deep commitment to human values, we can harness the power of AI to create a brighter future for all. Let us embark on this journey with optimism, curiosity, and a dedication to shaping AI for the benefit of humanity.

Thank you for purchasing this book! If you have enjoyed its content and have learned something new, please leave a book review rating on the website of purchase, and refer this book to a friend. Much appreciated!

For books on Blockchain Technology related topics, please check-out my other titles below:

1. Cryptocurrency Chronicles

Unlocking The Secrets Of Blockchain Technology

2. A Deep Dive Into The Top 50 Cryptocurrencies

A DYOR (Do Your Own Research) Guide

3. Common Crypto Investment Pitfalls and How To Avoid

A DYOR (Do Your Own Research) Guide

4. The Digital Revolution

Central Bank Digital Currencies (CBDC) Unveiled

5. Web 3.0

Unleashing The Power Of Decentralized Connectivity

6. Decentralized Finance (DeFi)

Unlocking The Future Of Financial Freedom